Happiness Chronicles

Short Stories and
Recipes for a Happy Life

www.TheWisdomBuffet.com

Copyright Notice

Dedication

This book is dedicated to you, our dear readers and to your happiness. It is our sincere intentions in writing this book that you achieve your own unique happiness.

Preface

In 2011, my whole world changed. What I thought of the world was far different than what I think of it today. It took a perfect storm of events to make me realize I had everything I could ever need or want in life. Why couldn't I realize it before – I often wonder when I think back.

The weeks leading up to the moment that changed my life, I was reading this book, The Master Key System by Charles F. Haanel, a turn of the century 'New Thought' writer. What's now a complete book, in 1916, it was broken up into twenty-four subsets or periodicals. It has action steps at the end of each subset on how to unlock the law of attraction and change your life forever.

My curiosity deepened after reading this passage in chapter nine, which you'll read in a moment. You see, my wife and I have a young child who was born with bi-lateral club feet. After his birth, we prayed and searched for the best doctors to help him. We were lucky and found the help he needed for his feet here in St. Louis. So when reading this part of the book it jumped out at me and made me pay very close attention.

The Master Key System by Charles F. Haanel – Part Nine

A letter from Frederick Andrews offers the following insight:

I was about thirteen years old when Dr. T. W. Marsee, since passed over, said to my mother: "There is no possible chance, Mrs. Andrews. I lost my little boy the same way, after doing everything for him that it was possible to do. I have made a special study of these cases, and I know there is no possible chance for him to get well."

She turned to him and said: "Doctor, what

would you do if he were your boy?" and he answered, "I would fight; fight, as long as there is a breath of life to fight for."

That was the beginning of a long drawn-out battle, with many ups and downs, the doctors all agreeing that there was no chance for a cure, though they encouraged and cheered us the best they could.

But at last the victory came, and I have grown from a little, crooked, twisted, cripple, going about on my hands and knees, to a strong, straight, well formed man.

Now, I know you want the formula, and I will give it to you as briefly and quickly as I can.

I built up an affirmation for myself, taking the qualities I most needed, and affirming for myself over and over again, "I am whole, perfect, strong, powerful, loving, harmonious and happy." I kept up this affirmation, always the same, never varying, till I could wake up in the night and find myself repeating, "I am whole, perfect, strong, powerful, loving, harmonious and happy." It was the last thing on my lips at night and the first thing in the morning.

Not only did I affirm it for myself, but for others that I knew needed it. I want to emphasize this point. Whatever you desire for yourself, affirm it for others, and it will help you both. We reap what we sow. If we send out thoughts of love and health, they return to us like bread cast upon the waters; but if we send out thoughts of fear, worry, jealousy, anger, hate, etc., we will reap the results in our own lives.

It used to be said that man is completely built over every seven years, but some scientists now declare that we build ourselves over entirely every eleven months; so we are really only eleven months old. If we build the defects back into our bodies year after year, we have no one to blame but ourselves.

Man is the sum total of his own thoughts; so the question is, how are we going to entertain only the good thoughts and reject the evil ones? At first we can't keep the evil thoughts from coming, but we can keep from entertaining them. The only way to do this is to forget them -- which means, get something for them. This is where the ready-made affirmation comes into play.

When a thought of anger, jealousy, fear or worry creeps in, just start your affirmation going. The way to fight darkness is with light -- the way to fight cold is with heat -- the way to overcome evils is with good. For myself, I never could find any help in denials. Affirm the good, and the bad will vanish.

- Frederick Elias Andrews

Approximately two years after reading these words from Frederick Elias Andrews in The Master Key System, I set out to find seven like-minded writing partners who were interested in exploring these ideas. Together, we are writing eight books, our collective wisdom on the affirmations listed in the above passage. I added 'healthy' to the affirmation, even though it may not be necessary, because I believe it's important in our day and age.

We call ourselves – The Wisdom Buffet Writers. Welcome to our first book: Happiness Chronicles – Short Stories and Recipes for a Happy Life.

Jim Thomas

Table of Contents

Preface 4

CH1-The Happiness Cookbook:
Recipes for a Balanced Life 13
By Mary Jane Kasliner

CH2- Finding Our Way To Happy 30
By Kim Klein

CH3- Finding Happiness Along The Tai Qi Gong Path .. 43
By Janet Mitsui Brown

CH4- Letting Go 56
By Katherine Graham

CH5- Bellaluna's Gift 74
By Belinda Mendoza

CH6- Lessons From David 87
By Mia Staysko

CH7- Secrets to Happiness 105
By Angi Ma Wong

CH8- Found in the Fall 133
By Jim Thomas

The Wisdom Buffet Writers 153
Biographies

The Happiness Cookbook

Recipes for a balanced life

By Mary Jane Kasliner

Are you starving for happiness? You're not the only one. The whole world is ravenous and waiting to sink their teeth into a fuller life.

Of course this is nothing new. The pursuit of happiness has driven mankind for centuries—and for centuries he has searched for the ideal ingredients to sustain his hunger pangs.

The Happiness Cookbook has age-old recipes for a blissful existence. Its recipes are simple and have been available for thousands of years. Many have tried to alter the ingredients with tempting substitutions, only to find that happiness eluded them. Taking advice from the ancient sages, this book provides the artificial and the authentic recipes. Decide for yourself.

Tempting Substitutions

The ego-driven recipes

Don't be fooled by the many ego-driven recipes for happiness. Sure they look tempting, but they will leave you craving something more. These recipes are nothing but a shell of what happiness is. Unfortunately, humankind has shown little willpower for resisting them.

The Fame Filler

"If you just set out to be liked, you will be prepared to compromise on anything at anytime, and would achieve nothing."

– Margaret Thatcher

Relatively new to the docket, this substitution has become one of the most popular recipes among those seeking happiness.

Ingredients:

- A one-parent family
- An attention-starved mind
- Fame, so millions can love you
- The approval of others

Directions:

Take equal parts of parental responsibility, and add to one parent. Slowly fold in overwhelming stress. Stir into a heaping level of attention deprivation, and mix in the desire for fame to fill the emptiness. Bake for a lifetime of seeking approval.

The Wealthy Wallet

"The love of family and the admiration of friends is much more important than wealth and privilege."

– Charles Kuralt

Okay, so who doesn't want wealth? It is a natural human desire. But what defines wealth, and how much money does it take to be happy? It depends on what your neighbor is cooking.

Ingredients:

- Self-comparison
- Keeping up with the Joneses
- More material possessions than your peers
- A burning hole in your wallet

Directions:

In a large saucepan, add self-comparison to keeping up with the Joneses. Simmer

until you burn a hole in your wallet,
and send yourself into the doldrums of
craving one desire after another.

Beauty Potion Number 9

"As soon as beauty is sought not from religion and love, but for pleasure, it degrades the seeker."

– Ralph Waldo Emerson

Beauty is in the eye of the beholder—or is it? Unfortunately, we are our own worst enemies when it comes to feeling good about how we look, and today, social media serves as a constant reminder for how we compare to others. This recipe is filled with faux ingredients that can deceive anyone into superficial happiness.

Ingredients:

- Flawless skin
- Silky straight hair
- Long eyelashes
- Pearly white teeth
- A perfect body

Directions:

In a large bowl, combine flawless skin, silky hair, long eyelashes, pearly whites, and a perfect body. Mix thoroughly. For best results, add photo-shopped, airbrushed, and other enhancements, and let simmer. Serves the ego until plastic surgery seems necessary.

The Know It All

"The key to success is to never stop learning. The key to failure is to think you know it all."

— Unknown

Wouldn't it be cool to be a genius for just one day? Maybe. But chances are that you will spend your entire life interacting with books rather than with people. This is a foolproof recipe for loneliness.

Ingredients:

- Research and study
- Pompousness
- Loneliness
- Playtime, family, and friends, optional

Directions:

Take equal parts research, study, and pompousness, and stir slowly until you alienate those who bring you joy. Yields a lifetime supply of loneliness.

The Power Roux

"Character is power."

– Booker T. Washington

This is one of the most enticing ego-driven recipes. The desire for power leads to unhappiness, and both the controller and the controlled are compromised.

Ingredients:

- Power over others
- Fear of losing power
- High stress
- Perfectionism

Directions:

Begin the power roux by mixing power over others with stress. Add the fear of losing power with having to do everything right. Be sure not to make any mistakes, and let simmer until misery sets in.

Authentic Recipes

Ingredients for a lifetime of happiness

For those who crave sustained happiness, these recipes comprise unerring advice from the ancient sages. No matter which guru you follow, each one has roamed the earth and has experienced the challenges and emotions that we do. The difference is that they consumed solely authentic recipes for happiness and stuck with them. These recipes call for unlimited amount of each ingredient to feed the soul.

The Buddha Delight

"We are shaped by our thoughts; we become what we think. When the mind is pure, joy follows like a shadow that never leaves."

– Buddha

This is a 2,500-year-old recipe from the Indian-Nepalese border. Take the following ingredients in abundance to sustain a happy state of being.

Ingredients:

- Daily meditation
- An unbiased view of all things
- Good deeds for others
- The absence of gossip
- Respect for others and for their property
- Follow-through on your word

Directions:

Add each ingredient into your life, and get to the bottom of your problems. Help others, and work toward your soul's mission. Do not pollute your mind with delusions. Allow ample time for these ingredients to simmer until they become part of your daily being. Consume them with joy.

Jesus Christ Bread of Life

"For what shall it profit a man, if he gain the whole world, and suffer the loss of his soul?"

– Jesus Christ

Aged since the first century in Judea, Jesus of Nazareth offers a simple recipe for rising to a life of happiness.

Ingredients:

- The meaning, importance, and satisfaction of life
- Kindness and compassion for others
- Love for thy neighbor
- Forgiveness
- A lifetime of joy
- Pleasure in your toils
- Happiness and blessedness within
- Belief in a higher being and higher self

Directions:

Sift out the physical ingredients, and add an abundance of love, kindness, and forgiveness. Cover with warmth and let rise. Bake in your heart and serve unto others.

All Natural St. Francis of Assisi

"For it is in giving that we receive."

– St. Francis of Assisi

From Assisi, Italy, this recipe offers profound advice for a simple and tranquil life.

Ingredients:

- The light in all things
- Good deeds daily
- Give to others
- Accept what is, let go of trying to change things
- Love where there is hate

- Faith where there is doubt
- Consolation and compassion for others in times of need

Directions:

Use a single sunbeam of light to drive away the shadows you encounter. Slowly add good deeds and giving to others. Add courage to change the things you can, and accept the things you cannot. Lower the heat, and let love and faith simmer for a steady tranquil life.

Socrates Stock

"He is richest who is content with the least, for content is the wealth of nature."

– Socrates

This recipe, sourced straight from Athens, offers unique insight into the history of happiness.

Ingredients:

- Connection with the soul
- A healthy portion of desire
- A peaceful mind
- A life of morality
- Unending virtue
- Crusading justice
- An expanded consciousness

Directions:

Add equal amounts of virtue and justice, and expand your consciousness twofold. Turn attention away from the body, and look towards the soul. Bring to a boil. See the good in yourself and in everyone else. Take an extra helping, and enjoy how sweet life can be.

The Daily Sweetener

"One of the sanest, surest, and most generous joys of life comes from being happy over the good fortune of others."

– Robert A. Heinlein

Presented to me by my meditation teacher Anmol Mehta, this recipe offers 10 simple ingredients for daily happiness.

Ingredients:

- Wake early
- Move the body enough to break a sweat
- Regular meditation
- Time in nature
- Completion of daily affairs
- Alone time
- Daily accounting
- One good deed a day
- Healthy entertainment
- A daily challenge

Directions:

Begin by rising early and get in touch with yourself. Simmer, and feel more focused throughout the day. Add a healthy portion of exercise to release toxins and keep your body in shape. Bring to a low boil while slowly adding daily meditation to cultivate a peaceful and open mind; strengthen the connection to your spirit. Let these ingredients cultivate your love for creation. Spend time in nature. Complete daily affairs by replacing procrastination with alone time without the distractions of your cell phone, computer, or TV.

As you bring the ingredients to a second boil, do some daily accounting. Reflect on your actions, words, and thoughts, especially in trying moments. Add a double serving of good deeds for others, and let it set for several minutes before adding entertainment. Finally, take on a new challenge. Consume daily, and this recipe will serve you for a lifetime.

So there you have it. I hope you will find that the simple things are what bring you the most joy in life, and there is no need to over-indulge in any one pleasure. Self-knowledge is a wonderful teacher. It can be a difficult process, but there is nothing more satiating than trying something new and gaining a more balanced and fulfilled life.

"Though difficult, we should try to cultivate non-attachment. Alone we come, alone we go. Non-attachment is happiness in this world."

– Dharma Teachings

Finding Our Way to Happy

By Kim Klein

"The talent for being happy is appreciating and liking what you have, instead of what you don't have."

– Woody Allen

Sounds simple, right? But happiness has been eluding mankind since the beginning of time, or at least since the Declaration of Independence asserted that we had the right to pursue it! And so, like an old-fashioned Easter egg hunt, we all scurried off to find it. And no matter how many eggs we found, there was always someone who found that extra egg, the perfect egg, the golden egg or the one filled with chocolate or money. And then, suddenly, all of our pretty pastel eggs just seemed to dim in comparison.

It seems that we may have the word "happy" confused with the word "perfect." For many of us, it seems that in order to be happy, things must be in perfect order. We must have the perfect relationship, the perfect home and the perfect career. But this is where the road to happiness can cause our vehicle to come to a screeching halt, when perfection and expectations, the mortal enemies of happy, all collide.

The main principal of the I Ching is that everything changes. This is the natural and universal law. Our moods and emotional state are not exempt from this law. When you study the Yin/Yang principal and their energetic polarities, you learn that everything has an opposite, that you can't have the light without the dark, the soft without the hard, and you definitely can't have the happy without the occasional sad. Resisting change and trying desperately to stay the same is what causes us pain, discomfort and unhappiness. Learning to flow and adapt to what is before us in the moment, and only this moment, is how we come to arrive at a place of peace, a place of happiness.

"The art of living does not consist in preserving and clinging to a particular mood of happiness, but in allowing happiness to change its form without being disappointed by the change; for happiness, like a child, must be allowed to grow up."

– Charles Langbridge Morgan

One of my teachers, Edgar Sung, told us once as he pointed to the Yin/Yang symbol, "Don't try to make everyone happy. You see the two halves? For as many people that will like what you do or who you are, there is always going to be that other side that does not. Accept this and let it go. Then, you can be happy."

"Folks are usually about as happy as they make their minds up to be."

– Abraham Lincoln

Don't worry; be happy. Just decide to be happy and voilà. Simple. But there are times when we really do want to be happy, but maybe there are things going on in our lives that truly warrant sadness. Our society doesn't like sadness. We've been told since we were little to "stop crying" or "quit being a baby" and that tears and sadness were the dead giveaways of a sissy, of someone weak, and therefore, less than. But we are humans and have been given many emotions to accompany our layered lives. We should feel all of these emotions at one time or another; we are wired to feel these things. Because a display of such emotion is unacceptable, it goes without saying that when we do show this side, our pain and our feelings become compounded with another emotion: guilt. Here in our country, we are expected to get over things rather quickly. We don't take the time necessary to mourn. And we feel guilty if we don't bounce back as expected and with a smile on our face. Get back to work, stay busy and keep the sadness at bay. People expect you to get back to normal within a very short time. We are quickly bombarded with questions and solutions. ("Are you dating yet? Come on, let me fix you up with Susie or Bill.") We need time to grieve our losses and adjust to changes. Accept it, feel it and sit with it, but know that everything changes, including this moment in time. This too will pass.

The Dalai Lama says, "My religion is kindness." Most of us would never treat the people we love or care about in such a shoddy manner as we treat ourselves. Just as you would support a friend or someone you love when they are going through a period of sadness or difficulty, don't give yourself any less. Be kind to yourself.

When happiness evades us and nothing seems to be going our way, it is time to turn it over to a greater power, to God, the universe, the great happiness giver in the sky or whomever you can relate to and believe in. Trust in the universe, in life, in yourself.

If we can wake up each morning and simply appreciate that we are still here and that we have been given another opportunity to explore, to find delight and beauty and to perhaps make a difference in someone else's life, that is a good start. Treat this day as if it is the only day you are given to be here and see how that mindset might make you choose happy over all other emotions that you could choose from. Stay present.

There was definitely a time when I thought that material possessions would lead to happiness. And I still do receive great joy in the moment of such acquisitions. At those times, I have a new found energy, my step becomes bouncier and my voice becomes more animated. But it is fleeting. I have learned that there is a big difference between those things that bring me true happiness and those things that bring me a momentary high.

So is it really happiness that we should be in pursuit of or the state of contentment, satisfaction and peace? One of my favorite quotes that I keep on my refrigerator as a constant reminder is: "Peace. It does not mean to be in a place where there is no noise, trouble or hard work. It means to be in those things and still be calm in your heart" (author unknown). We need to strive to do the same with the state of being happy.

"The future is no place to place your better days."

– Dave Matthews

Happiness – where in the world can we find it? They say that true happiness lies within, at the very core of our being. But for many of us, we don't understand that. How do we find it inside, and how do we go there? We don't know how to begin this journey to the land of happiness and feel we need a roadmap to find our treasure.

And we've all seen the map. It consists of things like meditation, exercise, bubble baths, puppies and happy children. But like happiness itself, this road map needs to be customized.

What happiness means to me might not be what happiness means to you. It's subjective. I had the incredible opportunity to meet the Dalai Lama in the early 80's.

I was unbelievably fortunate and also unbelievably naive, when I happened to be invited to meet the Dalai Lama at the home of a friend of my acupuncturist in Denver, Colorado. I was about 26 years old, and we all sat around in a circle in this ordinary living room, asking questions and waiting for the Dalai Lama's enlightened answers to our questions. I remember someone asking him the correct way to reach enlightenment. He smiled and gestured with his hands, "There is no one way to walk your spiritual path, there are many" he answered, and then advised us to go with what resonated with us the most. And I believe there is no one way to happiness, either.

You might find happiness living in a log cabin in the mountains, while I might find it living in a little beach cottage on Nantucket. But more important than where I live, or what physical objects surround me, is that

I find passion, joy, or maybe it is peace, with the people in my life, the work that I do and the things I create. Whether it's a simple piece of art, a healthy and beautifully prepared meal, my first morning cup of coffee, or the way I feel when I look at my daughter, these things are me. These feelings of happiness are a part of my core.

Just as important as the food we put into our mouths is the food we feed ourselves in the form of healthy relationships, our career or path in life, physical activity, our connection to nature and a spiritual practice. Knowing the path you are meant to be on, which is simply finding your passion, following it and trying to put into practice the suggestions below, for me, is the road to happiness:

Letting Go of Expectations - Trust. In the universe or trust in your God. Trust that life was given to you to live, fully.

Gratitude - Look at your life in smaller segments. Everything might not be going great in every life area, but if you break it down, you will find there are lots of things to be grateful for. Keep a gratitude journal. I will admit that there are days when the only thing I can find to write down is my morning cup of coffee. But hey, that is one thing I can always be grateful for, and sometimes, that's enough. And when we are grateful, when we consider life itself to be a blessing, we can't help but feel happy.

Be Present - On too many occasions, we wait for the right time and the right circumstances. We fall into the "as soon as I" syndrome. As soon as I lose 10 pounds, I'll go swimming in public. As soon as we replace the carpet, we'll have our friends over. When I think of how much time and enjoyment I have wasted while waiting for things to be "right," it's almost a sin. There is only right now, and right now is the right time to live the "right life."

Forgiveness - Anger and resentment only hurt the person bearing this poison. They do not harm the object of our anger. Give yourself a gift and let it go. Release the poison that is only poisoning you.

Passion - Find something you love to do, and, as Nike says, just do it. Even if you only take baby steps, just take that first step. If you feel there is nothing that truly interests you, reach back in your memory bank. As a child, what did you love to do? There is always some connection between the interests that we had as a child and what we would be passionate about doing as adults.

Sharing - Try a little experiment. Go out and buy yourself a little something, such as a new sweater or a tube of lipstick. It feels good, right? Now, go do something for someone else. Adopt a family at Christmas and give them a gift, the same sweater, freshly baked banana bread or your time. In which circumstance did that feeling of happiness last longer?

Acceptance - Wabi-sabi is the Japanese aesthetic or philosophy that finds beauty and acceptance in all things imperfect, impermanent and incomplete. It is the natural law of nature. Once we can accept that life is full of imperfections and that they too are beautiful and of no less value, we can relax our grip on the reins of perfection, expectations and outcomes.

When we accept that change is inevitable, that this is the way, the law of nature, and remember that we too are a part of nature, life becomes easier. We can then get in and flow with the current instead of struggle to swim upstream.

Finding Happiness Along the Tai Qi Gong Path

By Janet Mitsui Brown

Can you recall the last time you were happy? Can you describe it in detail? Can you recall the joy, and how it felt? Did you have the patience and fortitude to sit in silence and enjoy the moment?

I'm lucky because I must admit, I have my fair share of happiness. I recall it sometimes in moments of serenity – that refreshing taste of the best ice cream at the right moment; a magical first kiss; placement glow when winning a contest. Smiles and inner radiance. Sheer bliss.

And how does this happiness come to be? Is it personal delight as a result of an outside happenstance? The perfect combination of sugar & cream? The spontaneity of two lips meeting? An award acknowledging my worth?

As time passes, I find I am eager for happiness that is not dependent on other things, events or people.   I just want to smile because I'm healthy and here in this moment -- alive and breathing in life force energy -- enjoying the environment and the world around me.   When happiness comes from an external occurrence because of timing, hard work, and occasionally luck, there's a dependence on some thing, or person, or act to make it happen. But when happiness comes from within, it comes from the confidence, persistence, and some discipline to remember its birthright. I have the power to make happiness happen. And I can make it happen often.   This is the kind of happiness I want for me, and now for you.

When happy now, I am in tune with my "self," unconditionally, with no pressure to be someone other than who I am, unforced. When happy, I can hear and feel my heart in radiant bliss. And it can happen every day.

My secret is this: my personal happiness comes through my daily practice of Tai Qi Gong exercises. Through daily discipline and returning to my practice if I miss a day or two, I have come to know happiness.

Yes. You, too, will find happiness along the Tai Qi Gong path.

What is Tai Qi Gong?

Qi Gong originated from historic rituals with spiritual connections – the concept of gathering sacred elements daily to heal. The goal was to allow the self to blossom naturally, as earth intended. The practice enables the body and nervous system to be put into a relaxed state with its repetition in motion and time, improving our physical and psychological well-being and spiritual insight.

Tai Chi is a natural extension of Qi Gong. It developed into a simple series of movements, yet it retained Qi Gong's healing gifts.   Recent scientific studies indicate that Tai Chi improves balance, calms, and then focuses the mind in physical meditation resulting in healing and empowerment. A trained Tai Chi sifu (teacher) , regardless of size, can skillfully defend against another, demonstrating power in defense and discipline.

Scientists have proven through brain scans that practicing qi gong and tai chi leads to steady brain flow, and increased brain activity in the left prefrontal lobes.

From the writings of Sanbao (Buddha, Dharma & Sangha):

"Everyone is born with Qi (energy), and if used daily (gong), you will reinforce your left prefrontal lobes steadily. The prefrontal cortex plans cognitive behavior, personality, decision-making and moderates social behavior - the orchestration of thoughts and actions in concert with internal goals. Western science can explain what qi gong

can do but innately you will truly discover strength, empowerment, and spirituality after doing tai qi gong - first qi gong then tai chi, on a daily basis. With this comes the serenity of bliss - also known as happiness."

The practice of Tai Qi Gong begins with Qi Gong exercises and flows into the form of Tai Chi. This combined practice brings together the health and spiritual benefits of both forms of energy work in a unique blend, taking you on a path to happiness. The goal of practicing Tai Qi Gong is the cultivation of unconditional happiness. It is Happiness that is manufactured organically, independent of outside forces, people, and things.

Through the practice of Tai Qi Gong we learn the following on the Path to Happiness:

- To stand straight is to be confident and balanced.

- To breathe slowly is to find one's breath.
- As the mind becomes quiet, and the breath steadies, the body slows down.
- Let qi flow in the body naturally.
- The flowing body movement helps one to be in sync with the environment.
- Tai Chi Gong cultivates strength.
- The mind will reflect the environment, accepting joyfully life as it naturally unfolds.

To embark on this path to happiness, begin by practicing Qi Gong followed by Tai Chi. This combined Tai Qi Gong leads you down the path, but remember it is a journey, not a destination. The philosophy of Tai Qi Gong teaches us all -- when man, woman, earth and heaven align, everyone and every thing benefits.

Gift Yourself With Joy

Gift yourself with 15 minutes a day to practice 9 simple exercises to begin your journey on the path to happiness through Tai Qi Gong.

Set aside 15 minutes for yourself. It can be any time of day, but it's best if you choose a consistent time each day. Find a place you are comfortable – it might be outdoors, or perhaps the family room or somewhere else you feel at ease in your home. This is your time, so make sure there are no interruptions. If you like, do this with others – but keep talking to a minimum. Enjoy the silence.

- To begin, stand tall with your legs slightly apart and hands at your sides, resting lightly on your outer thighs. You may have quiet, peaceful background music if you like, or simple silence. It's blissful to listen to the environment, even in an urban setting.

- Breathe quietly in and out 9, 18, or 27 times. Begin with 9, and then gradually increase the number.

- Tap your fingers on your head 9 times. Between taps, move your hands quickly away from your head and hear the popping sounds. Tap your head again in two more sets of 9 times each for a total 27 taps.

- Climb an imaginary ladder to the sky by moving your hands and feet at the same time as if climbing a celestial ladder. Keep your hands no higher than eye level. You can hum or chant while doing this. This exercise adjusts your qi (or chi) and benefits your internal organs.

- Cross an imaginary spiritual bridge

with both hands together barely touching, as in prayer or meditation, in front of your lower face and moving them side to side while keeping your head steady. Move your feet by stepping forward and backward. This takes concentration and focus so imagine you are crossing abridge from earth to sky, moving your hands sideways and your feet forward & back.

- Enter an imaginary space with your elbows bent inward and your palms facing outwards, matching the direction you are gazing at. Move your palms in a circular motion first one way and then in the opposite direction. If doing this with a partner, you can walk and turn to this person; then you can both feel each other's palms without touching.

Notice the qi (chi).

- Press your nostrils together to improve your sense of smell – count to 9, 18 or 27.

- Place the palms of your hands facing each other but apart and move them in and out in front of your nose and mouth – do this 9, 18 or 27 times. Notice what you smell. Concentrate on the numbers and the smell only.

- Immerse yourself in a spiritual rain. Start with your hands at your sides but a distance from your outer thighs. Wiggle your fingers and lift your palms upward as you gather the rain. As you move them up, you can move around as long as your arms remain stretched with your fingers wiggling. Feel the qi energy around you. Continue to wiggle your fingers as you bring your hands down in front of your face, palms emitting the energy towards you with fingers wiggling, and then back down to your sides in the beginning position. Do this 9 times.

- Massage your arms without touching them. Go around your shoulders and your entire body. Do this 9 times -- you are massaging the qi energy emanating from your body.

- Find your dan tien (the center of your energy field). It is an area two sideways finger lengths below your belly button. Place your hands over your dan tien, lightly touching the body, the left over your right hand for females and your right over your left for males. Rub this area in circular motions barely touching your body, at least 9 times. You are energizing yourself.

- Close this session by breathing quietly in and out 9 times. Shake your feet and hands to let go of residual negative energy. Now stand balanced on both feet, and let the palms of your hands face the sky, at your sides or in front of you – your preference. Take this time to let in powerful new energy from heaven and earth – let your clock stand still. Smile and enjoy this happy moment.

Now you can get on with your day. Take a moment during the next 24 hours to remember the Tai Qi Gong exercise. I hope you will smile because you have taken your time to be joyful.

The practice of Tai Qi Gong in the global world has arrived, and its health and maturity depend on all of us who practice it. You will find your own markers on the Tai Qi Gong path to happiness that let you know you are on the right course. Notice the markers. Appreciate them. You will know when you smile; it will be because you simply feel good. Allow this to propel you further on the continuing path to Happiness.

Letting Go

By Katherine Graham

"The most important thing is to enjoy your life—to be happy—it's all that matters."

– Audrey Hepburn

I have one chance to get this right. And then they're gone.

Would my children want to run home to me or run far, far from me? This is the thought that seared through my mind after seeing my daughter cringe from me. I had yelled, raged really, over some very minor thing. Perhaps it was the fact she had gotten distracted ("Can't you focus on one thing?") or taken too long to get her shoes on ("How can you lose your shoes, you just took them off!") This innocent, sweet child who I loved more than anything. The shame was palpable, deep. How had yelling at a three and six-year-old this way become acceptable behavior? Was this really my version of successful parenting? To be a raging, nagging, annoyed, frustrated mother? Was this what successful, happy people did?

I had just taken my consulting business to the next level. I was in the middle of writing my first book, building a platform, always on my phone and computer, obsessed with tracking new Twitter followers. I had but three precious, uninterrupted hours to accomplish all of this while my children were in school. I was utterly annoyed with having to stop the important work I was doing to sit in carpool, and then rush to ballet and piano, cook dinner, clean bottoms and brush teeth. Not to mention the laundry. Such mundane household chores had become the Boogeyman, keeping me from my greater life's purpose. Keeping a nice home for my family held little reward.

I would wipe the same counter, sweep the same floor and do the same tedious routine all over again tomorrow.

Fulfilling my role as a mother and wife had simply become a daily annoyance. It was getting in the way of what I wanted to accomplish, my goals, my vision. This annoyance carried through to how I treated my kids, my husband and neglected friends. These are hard sentences to write.

My lean-in generation of mothers promised me I could "have it all." I didn't have to choose between motherhood and career. If I was smart, organized and motivated enough, I could do both. The overriding message being women who only stayed home with their children were doing not only themselves, but also society at large, a disservice by taking their talents out of the pool. Besides, it was dangerous and naive to depend solely on a man to provide and care for you. While I can tell you this is a big, fat lie, I did my best to deny it for some time. Instead of looking within to find my own version of success, I looked to the left and to the right of me. I gave in to societal pressure to prove that I could be the do-it-all-Mom and became overwhelmed, on edge and unhappy in the process. It was a mid-life awakening.

Hot and cold, light and darkness, good and bad, happiness and unhappiness. Seemingly opposing concepts, yet simply two sides of the same mountain. I had gotten a taste of the dark side of the mountain through driving myself to live someone else's version of success. I was ready for the bright side of the mountain. I was ready to be happy.

When I was growing up, happiness was mostly described in terms of "success." Success in school meant getting good grades, which made my parents happy. Success in social circles meant knowing the right people and advancing your character and standing through networking and nurturing relationships. Success in career meant having single-minded focus and ambition and the desire to be the best. I was taught that if you followed the normal path to success, you would be happy. For the most part, this normal path usually looked a little something like this: you are born - preschool - elementary school - high school - college - career - marriage - mortgage - kids - mid-life crisis - retire - die. Avoid divorce; throw in a dog, maybe buy a fancy car and you were right in the mainstream view of a successful life.

Often, the first step to getting happy is to simply let go of the things that make you unhappy. For me it was letting go of the illusion of perfection, of being the woman who can do it all. I let go of the ambition that made me ugly. The burning desire to chop my own wood led me to view my family as a distraction instead of my single greatest priority.

I let go of my ego-driven obsession with growing a successful start-up. I had already given birth to two start-up ventures that needed a mother, a guide and a role model. I was already in the best business there was, yet my version of success was so out of whack I was failing at all things at once.

When we are constantly banging our heads against something, either it or our mindset around it needs to change in order to find peace and contentment. I learned the lesson in the pain. Instead of spreading myself thin, I dropped a lot and ended up gaining so much more. No longer pulled in a million directions, each day with my sweet girls became a profound gift. In order to be fully present in my life, I underwent a digital detox and wriggled out of the net that bound me. I stopped taking my phone everywhere I went. I left it behind while going on walks with my dogs, once again enjoying the quiet time alone with my thoughts and just being in nature, looking up at the sky instead of down on a tiny screen. I don't plan to ever go back.

I inched my way to complete and utter contentment with my life through mindset shifts. For me, these were:

Expectation

It's good to have standards and work toward the best outcome. But expectation is different. Expectation is the self-centered presumption that someone or something will, and should, behave, act, respond or produce according to your predetermined needs, wants or desires. It is the result of an "it's all about me" mindset. Expectation leads you to ignore certain blessings in your life because they don't look, feel, or smell just the way you thought. In this way, it sets you up for failure and certain disappointment. The deeper self knows the anguish such expectations cause, yet we cling to them as though they were the coffee fueling our successes. Expectation is the smog that covers happiness.

I have clients who are deeply unhappy because they expected to be somewhere they are not, earning _____ amount by some previously established stage in life. Their parents, spouse, friends expected more of them. I expected to have my book written by such and such date. Your employees can never seem to live up to your expectation. The men your girlfriend meets are never what she expected. Your brother is never happy with life because he did not get the job/car/wife he expected.

Others are not here to live up to your expectations. And you are not here to live up to theirs.

Being in control of my own happiness, I stopped expecting things. I hoped, worked, planned, and prayed for things. But I no longer expected my children, my computer, the flow of traffic or my spouse, to read my mind and instantly deliver to my exacting standards. I stopped expecting life, people, and things to fit my invented notions and began enjoying things as they were.

Perspective

"We can complain because rose bushes have thorns, or rejoice because thorn bushes have roses."

– Abraham Lincoln

Your perspective on life is possibly the greatest indicator of the amount and quality of joy in your life. Having a Happiness Perspective requires humility, sometimes blind optimism and an overarching sense of humor. Humor allows us to keep an intellectual perspective on life. Look around and you can find the humor in just about every aspect of life. The interesting characters you encounter. The way certain things do what they do. Everyone and everything is potentially humorous in some way.

When I was younger, my mother would take me to the mall to sit and people-watch for hours. She would make up names, concoct elaborate relationships and weave complex life stories for the people shopping, eating and talking around us. We had nicknames for all of our neighbors and imagined them in all kinds of humorous episodes. We weren't vicious or demeaning, just having fun and finding humor by looking out for the unexpected within the norm; the eccentricities, the shades of color around us. The world was our soap opera.

A Happiness Perspective also requires not taking things too seriously and never personally. One of the quickest routes to unhappiness is taking other's actions as an assault, insult or negative statement about you. If something did not go my way, I would think, "Why are they doing this TO ME?" Now I know others' attitudes, expressions, beliefs, words, deeds and actions always stem from, and are a direct reflection of, them. Never, ever, ever, ever are things about you. Your boss is a grump and having a bad day; don't take it personally. Your spouse needs space and seems a little quiet; don't take it personally. Some stranger treats you miserably; not your problem. In this way, you deflect other people's junk instead of taking it on as your own. Picture yourself like a duck that lets it all roll off your back, like so much water.

Having a Happiness Perspective does not

allow life's fluff to get in the way of your personal contentment. It does not give your power away so easily.

Whenever I need a dose of perspective, I think of the unending intricacies of life and nature. That my body functions in incredibly complicated systems that I need not program, nor do much to maintain, other than breathe, eat clean food, and sleep. That we are riding on a hot ball rotating in expansive space. I remember the fleetingness of all things and that all things change. I remember that I will never be this youthful or have the exact set of circumstances, or opportunities before me. That the world is basically good and everyone in it, just a little mad.

Boundaries

Overwhelm, unhappiness and the sinking feeling that your life is spiraling out of control is clear indication that your boundaries are either thin or broken. This occurred to me when I noticed the men in my life never seemed to suffer the same way that most modern women do. They don't cram their schedules so full to tend and befriend and carry out a million tiny tasks. Men choose a role and hold their boundaries. They delegate. They don't attempt to be everything to everyone, all at once.

Through this realization, I learned the power and freedom of guilt-free boundaries through confidently using one little word: "No!" My sister in the ministry calls it the "Holy No!" (As in the opposite of Hell, Yes!) By saying no and refusing to take on things that ultimately sabotage your success and happiness; you are honoring yourself, your family, and God. School committees, garden club fundraisers, charities, your church, the opportunities for giving of your time are endless. Saying no sets and protects your boundaries and is often the easiest way to say yes to yourself. Consider it a service to God that the proposed job can now go to someone who will give it the passion and service it truly deserves.

Strong boundaries come down to GIGO = put Good In, you'll get Good Out. Protect your happiness through filtering your daily inputs. Don't watch the news before bed. Play beautiful music instead. Read uplifting books, watch funny movies. Cut the ties to people or things that sap you, or make you feel "less than."

Trust

This was most difficult for me. My own father left my mother when I was eighteen

months old. I was the youngest of four
children and my mother had few options.
We struggled. Fast forward thirty years
and I lacked trust in my own marriage. I
held the deep belief that it was foolish and
extremely naive for any woman, especially
one with young children, to rely fully on
another human to protect their future
security and interests.

You do not learn to trust. You simply
make up your mind to do it.

In full trust, I embraced the immense,
loving support of my husband, like falling
onto a mattress. I verified that my updated
version of success was the outward
expression and manifestation of my inner
truth and purpose for living. While I
continue to bump into driving personal
ambition, I trust that all will get done,
in the right time and at the right place. I
trust the wisdom of the universe and the
unfolding of plans.

My attitude about daily chores has gone from annoyance to being immensely grateful that I have a beautiful home to care for, and the health with which to do it. I like to feel the strength of my arms as I carry loads of laundry to my bed to fold, and picture my love going into the folds of the clothes so that it carries through to the precious people who wear them. Like a constant feedback mechanism, the people I love the most reflect back to me what I put out to the world. And what I get back now feels like a big, gold star on my homework.

If you are unhappy, overwhelmed, or feel pulled in a million directions, it is time to assess your version of success. Is it built around your own personal energy level, passions, desires and priorities? If you were to write it down and read it out loud, would you hear only your voice? While writing this I asked a friend what her version of success was. She thought for a few moments. When she delivered her thoughts, her voice changed. When I pointed this out she replied, "You're right. That's not me. That is what my Dad thinks." Often we take on other people's versions of success as our own without thinking about it. Often we find we've lived half our life going after what someone else wanted.

A wise friend once wrote a letter to herself. It was from her future seventy-year-old self. It said to guard her personal happiness with the ferocity of a snow leopard. For within this was the secret to her life's purpose. When she was in pain, this was a clue. When she was unhappy, it was a sign that she had veered. The letter said to garden more. That she was most powerful when she was quiet. That the key to success and happiness was written on her heart. All she need do was dig deep and discover what was already there. She

would know she was on the right path
when she woke up each day truly, deeply,
thoroughly happy.

Bellaluna's Gift

By Belinda Mendoza

What is happy-ness and what does it mean to you? I learned this the hard way. I lost the most precious thing in my life a few years ago, my beloved yorkie, Bellaluna. I journaled throughout my painful grief, and turned my writings into a sweet book, Feng Shui for Healing the Loss of a Pet, Restoring Balance During Grief and Loss, a Personal Journey.

Through my Feng Shui practice, I have become a Taoist (pronounced "Dow," like the Dow Jones) due to its simplicity. I believe the simpler our lives are, the happier we are. The Tao is the philosophy on which feng shui is based. It has to do with our connection to nature and the duality of life, yin and yang, sadness and happiness. I experienced the happiest times with my Bella. When she died, I realized what happiness means to me personally. The inner peace, contentment, and moments of pure joy with Bella created that amazing feeling. I love being a pet owner. I find that pets offer keys to happiness:

Pets Give Unconditional Love

I wondered why it was so difficult when my dog passed away. Yes, I was sad not having her anymore. I know now that my loss was more complex than simple sadness. Bella was the only being in my life at the time offering me unconditional love. No one ever greeted me at the door to my home with such excitement and happiness…EVERY TIME! It didn't matter if I scolded her for something, she would still return to that loving, sweet state of joy and lick it all over me. She brought out my compassion. After watching me with Bella one day, a friend said, "I've not seen this truly loving side of you before."

Pets Always Live in the Present Moment

They are like little "Zen masters." In meditation practice we learn to cultivate inner peace, which leads to happiness. There are no better teachers than pets. They remind us to stop and breathe. Presently, I share my life with two yorkies, Bodie and Gracie Bell. When I work for hours on the computer, my little dogs wag their tails and either bark or push my leg, alerting me to take a break. This cue means it is time to take them for a long walk and focus on "walking meditation." Taking time just to walk, without being distracted by the phone or stopping to visit with people or places brings me back to the calm, centered state of the present moment which I share with my dogs.

Pets Don't Hold Grudges

Pets don't remember the last frustration or

anger you expressed. Unlike humans, they return the love they receive immediately and come back to the present moment. Only people hold grudges. But have you seen a happy person who holds a grudge? A grudge is stuck energy that is being held in the body. It harms the person who holds it. I am reminded of this daily when I see my dogs playing. Whenever I feel a grudge coming on, I give my dogs a big hug, take a deep breath, and let go.

Pets Provide Laughter

I have never laughed more than with my pets. Whether it is something funny they do on their own or while I am teaching them tricks, they remind me to laugh and this adds to my happiness quotient. Medical doctor, Mehmet Oz said on one of his shows that laughter can lower blood pressure, increase serotonin levels (feel good transmitters), and decrease depression.

"Your sense of humor is one of the most powerful tools you have to make certain that your daily mood and emotional state support good health."

– Paul E. McGhee, Ph.D.

Who needs drugs? I attend many canine events, dress my dogs up at Halloween, get their photos taken, and do fun things year round.

Pets Always Forgive

Like not holding on to a grudge, forgiveness is a key to being a happy person. I find that when I have not forgiven someone, I hold back in other areas of my life. It is as though the heart has a door that says, "Closed." Pets love you no matter what! Treat them well and they will offer you joy and happiness their whole lives. When Bella died, I did not feel I could get another pet. I was so sad and I felt guilty about her passing. A tape ran over and over in my mind: "If I had done something different, would she still be with me?" I couldn't forgive myself in the beginning. Yet, I did heal with time and support. I still miss her, but most of the time; I feel joy when I think of her. I found comfort reading the words of "The Rainbow Bridge Poem" that can be found on many Humane Society websites:

... As much as I loved the life we had and all the times we played, I was so very tired and knew my time on earth would fade. So whenever you need to find me, we're never far apart. If you look beyond the Rainbow and listen with your heart...

– author unknown

Once I forgave myself and came to understand that there was nothing I could do to change things, I adopted two new furry yorkies, Bodhi and Graciebell, who are my current loves. They helped me to open my heart again. Many people who have lost pets, adopt new ones, and lose again. They continue to adopt because they are offering service to another pet, who in turn, helps them open up their hearts to more joy. Dog expert Cesar Milan says over 4 million dogs are euthanized each year in the U.S. alone. Adopt a pet to help this situation and bring happiness back into your life.

Pets open up your heart chakra.

I like this beautiful quote by W. Bruce Cameron.

> *"Dogs come into our lives to teach us about love, they depart to teach us about loss. A new dog never replaces an old dog: it merely expands the heart. If you have loved many dogs your heart is very big."*

Opening up your heart chakra promotes happiness. In our bodies, we have seven chakras (energy centers) that keep us functioning and whole. The crown, third eye, throat, heart, solar plexus, sexual, and root chakras are where we store our emotions. They have colors and vibrations. They are said to all be "spinning" at the same time when in balance. A meditation teacher of mine said that all we have to do while sitting is to visualize each chakra and "SMILE." This alone would balance the chakras and bring contentment.

I enjoy doing healing work on my dogs, as I am an energy practitioner. A well-known psychic told me that I was a healer of pets in a past life. In this lifetime my soul wants me to work on people. While I do work on people, I prefer to work on pets for all the reasons I discuss in this chapter. While some people use prayer with intentions or just simple prayer, my modality is Reiki. I place my hands on my pet's belly, head, or back and allow the energy to flow from my hands to them in just the right amounts. There is an innate intelligence that knows just what is needed. I can tell that my dogs feel the loving energy because they immediately calm down, relax, and even fall asleep. My female yorkie snores, which tells me it's working! This healing energy balances my dogs' chakras and mine as well because the energy has to flow through me in order to get to them. I mention this because one of the key ways to feel happiness is through service to others. Sometimes we struggle to stop our inner turmoil and change our state of mind. Moving out of ourselves by serving others can bring healing and joy. (Give your pet a massage when feeling out of sorts.)

Pets Bring Out the Child in Us

No child was ever born to be a scrooge. Assuming all basic needs are being met, if unhappy, the child is learning this from the people with whom they live. I read once that up to the age of five years, children believe everything they see or hear. Think for a moment how it feels to be a child… playful, innocent, creative, inquisitive, daring, confident, fearless, loving, and fully in the present moment.

These words also describe animals. I am always thinking of ways to entertain and have fun with my two yorkies. They force me out of my shell, to get exercise, to meet new people. For the past five years I have helped organize a dog group. I observe how some owners are depressed or have low energy when they arrive. By the end of our meet up, they are smiling and enjoying themselves, watching their dogs play.

Pets Bring Life Into a Physical Space

In my Feng Shui practice, I help people set up personal spaces for serenity and peace. Maybe you struggle with how to achieve happiness. Setting up a space to reflect the feeling you desire is a great start. I love the work of authors and spiritual teachers, Jerry and Esther Hicks, who wrote "Ask and It Is Given". They are very clear that you must create a happy feeling in order to manifest what you want. In ancient China, palaces were magnificent in design and decor and the emperors kept deer on their grounds. They felt these animals brought them good luck. In the art of Feng Shui, it is said that if you have healthy, happy animals, you will invite abundance and joy into your life.

Pets Don't Fight Balance

Go for the happy feeling in every moment. This is what animals do. Do what you can to move from one state to another. If working at your computer and feeling depressed, play some of your favorite music and dance. Take a friend you enjoy spending time with out to lunch. Whether it is to sleep, play, or just be, animals always search for the "good space." They let you know when things are not working for them, but they find their own equilibrium. My dogs let me know when they want to play. When my female wants a back rub, she comes to sit on my lap. She looks up adoringly at me until I begin the massage. Pets don't fret about anything. If they are fearful or nervous about something they are experiencing, these feelings don't last long. Before long they are back to playing and having fun.

Having lost a pet, I value the precious times with my current ones. My happiness has been restored. I wrote a letter to Bella when she passed on. It was not a sad letter, but one of wishing her well and for a peaceful passing. I wished her joy on her new journey. I wanted my future memories of her to be of the happy times. I could see how life is a sacred circle.

My Dear Bella:

You brought so much joy, love, and laughter to my life. No pet will ever replace you. You are missed for your constant companionship, unconditional love, and never-ending affection. You taught me so much about being in the present moment, being spontaneous, playful, patient, affectionate, and most of all about love. You made me so happy. I wish you joy in your new life.

You will be forever in my heart.

Love,
Your Mom

Lessons from David

By Mia Staysko

David started out like most of us, a pretty normal kid. However, from all accounts, he had a bit of a nasty, mean streak as a kid, a personality trait that persisted right up until the night that changed everything.

My husband Steve, an absolute bear of a man, hated his older brother growing up. Dave, though smaller, was mean and opinionated. He made no bones about voicing his opinion, about everything and everybody. He got into fights often and his younger brothers were easy targets. He had an attitude, a real chip on his shoulder.

Even in adulthood you walked on eggshells around him. He could be your best friend one moment, and at the flip of a coin, something about him would turn and he'd be at your throat, sometimes literally. His temper was legendary. He was hard on his kids. He was hard on his wife. He was probably hard on his employees. Dave was tough.

At 50, Dave, an overworked executive at a large paving company, was overcome one night with a massive headache. After heading into the bathroom, he collapsed to the floor. His wife called for an ambulance. Inside his brain, an aneurism the size of a pinkie finger had formed. It would ultimately change him forever.

That was nearly 15 years ago and the road to recovery has been long and arduous both for David and for his family. He has had to relearn everything to some degree. Many friends have gone by the wayside, as often happens in these situations. To their credit, his wife and family have stayed beside him all the way, despite the difficulty sometimes in doing so.

Dave has aphasia. An acquired

communication disorder, aphasia affects one's ability to communicate effectively, but has no effect on intelligence. Dave is as smart and as capable as ever, but he cannot, for example, read a simple sentence. He cannot calculate change in a financial transaction. He must be carefully shown a task, sometimes over and over again, until his brain makes a more permanent connection and remembers.

However, despite all that he has been through, despite all of his day-to-day challenges, my brother in law Dave is a happy person - perhaps the happiest person I know. He is seldom without a smile.

It begs the question: how can someone with so many challenges, so much to be potentially unhappy about, be happy? What is happiness anyway? Are some born happier than others? Can we, as we are led to believe, buy happiness? How do we get happy?

I believe that happiness is cumulative. When the individual moments that bring us joy, contentment, love, peace and other positive emotions, outweigh the moments that bring us sadness, grief, stress and other negative emotions, we end up with a happy life. Every life has times of happiness, and times without it.

Happiness is individual and subjective as well. What makes you happy is not necessarily what will make me happy. It is important not to believe that some particular thing could make anybody happy.

We each must pursue our own individual brand of happiness.

Despite what the media would like us to believe, you can't buy happiness. While attaining certain goals, or getting things that we desire can definitely bring us moments of joy, these are simply moments, fleeting and impermanent.

You'd have to spend a lot of cash to buy enough of those moments to add up to a lifetime of happiness!

I also believe that some are just born with a happier disposition than others. Nature and nurture most definitely play a part.

I've thought a lot about Dave and why he is so happy. It has occurred to me that perhaps it is unfair to compare him to so-called "normal" people. After all, he is a brain-injured person. His life situation and his perspective are different from other people. However, we all have individual lives and perspectives, and to consider the happiness of a brain-injured, or otherwise different person, to be of lesser quality or importance than yours or mine is unfair. A child has a different experience than an adult, they have less responsibility and fewer worries, but I do not believe their happiness is any less significant than mine.

It has been interesting to watch Dave relearn certain things and make new brain connections. Anyone familiar with a brain-injured person knows that they have their own special way of expressing themselves and that they phase in and out of certain stages and sayings. Dave often, out of the blue, will come up with a new saying. We call them "Dave-isms" in our family.

In David's case it seems, at least on the surface, that happiness is not a part of his genetic make-up, or if it is, his life circumstances may have played a part in hiding his naturally joyful expression. In this way in particular I think that Dave has much to teach about becoming happier since his happiness seems to be a learned way of being. By reflecting on his attitude, his new, softer demeanour, I think that there are several ways of expressing ourselves – "Dave-isms" that all of us could adopt. Perhaps in doing so, we could all increase our happiness.

Go Inward - "Mind yourself"

"It is not easy to find happiness in ourselves, and it is not possible to find it elsewhere."

– Agnes Repplier

Dave spends a lot of time immersed in his own thoughts. He struggles with crowds, as his brain can't process multiple conversations all at one time. He is best one on one. He spends a lot of time in silence, and only speaks when he is ready.

Most of us could stand to spend more time immersed in our own thoughts. Instead we are immersed in noise. We have conversations with little meaning; online with people we don't really even know. We talk too much and listen too little. Perhaps more often, we should "mind ourselves" and worry less about the activities of others.

Studies show that people who meditate,

who go inward on a regular basis are happier overall.

Be Present – "I forgot"

Communication, for most of us, requires a sense of the past and of the future. We have conversations with the assumption that the other person has both some basic background knowledge and the ability to figure out where we are going with our topic. Although Dave certainly has vast knowledge floating around in his brain in the same way that the rest of us do, he doesn't always have instant access to it, or at least the ability to easily communicate it. Talking to Dave is a bit like playing charades. You figure out first what general topic you think might be on his mind, and then you must listen attentively and try to piece together the story. Because his thoughts do not always connect in a linear fashion he can be in the middle of a conversation and then suddenly lose it.

The train simply goes off the rails and he has to take a few moments, sometimes longer, to search his brain's database for the path he was on when he started. 'I forgot' is a common phrase and one has to be prepared to pay attention and to pick up where he left off when the train gets back on track. It can be frustrating for both parties. Patience is required.

Though he certainly thinks about the past and the future, he is most often "right here, right now" and being with him requires you to be right here with him. You must be fully present to chat with Dave. You have to stop what you are doing, and listen attentively so you can help him to fill in the blanks. It is an art which most of us are not practiced in.

Fighting with David is an exercise in self-torture. Imagine you have an argument and the person you've fought with forgets all about it. Really forgets, not just that placating "I don't remember" that most of us practice. You find yourself going over and over something that happened hours or even days ago and they have completely forgotten it. They have moved on while you have emotionally remained in the fight. Who do you think is happier about your relationship?

We spend the vast majority of our time reliving the past and fretting about the future rather than just being here, now. If you are stressed about something, take a moment to take stock and be present. Ask yourself if what you are fussing about is actually happening in this very moment. If it is, deal with it, if it isn't just acknowledge that and let it go. We may discover that 90% of what makes us unhappy isn't even happening right now. Release it and find something to be grateful for instead.

Gratitude - "I was dead"

Dave is grateful. He seldom speaks of it but like, I suspect, many who have survived a life threatening illness, he lives it. He is acutely aware that he could have died just as easily as lived and that each day is a gift. He wakes up happy and he goes to bed content. Every day after his aneurism is God-given.

It is hard to be unhappy when we are grateful. When we begin a sentence with "thank you for…" it is difficult to add a "but" to our sentence. Gratitude is perhaps the biggest single contributor to our overall happiness.

I love the story of Jesus asking his disciples to give bread and fish to his followers after they travelled to see him. He knew he did not have enough. He thanked God for what he had anyway and enough soon appeared. Regardless of your religious or spiritual beliefs there is a lesson to be learned in this Biblical story. Be thankful, for even "not enough" is something, and often more than someone else might have. When we are thankful, we draw attention to what we have rather than to what we don't have and when we reflect on what we have, it makes us happy.

Environment Counts - "I'm going farther"

Dave spends a lot of time alone, in nature, in the pristine mountains of British Columbia. The air is fresh, the water clean. Nature has great Feng Shui.

Dave is an avid outdoorsman. He spends his summers in pursuit of bass, his spring chopping deadfall for his wood stove, his summer in the garden, and his fall hunting for game, which in some small way contributes to his family's larder. He knows the natural order of things. He understands life and death. When something is bothering Dave, he goes up "farther" into the sunshine, and he comes back refreshed and content.

The quality of the environment in which you spend time has a profound effect on both the mind and the body. Environments that are in disarray or chaotic, ugly or uncared for, tend to attract circumstances that reflect that same energy. Surrounding yourself as much as possible with things that are natural, beautiful and orderly can contribute to your overall happiness.

Purpose - "I work all the time"

"We act as though comfort and luxury were the chief requirements of life, when all that we need to make us really happy is something to be enthusiastic about."

– Charles Kingsley

When he first had his aneurism there was a difficult period of time in which Dave was entirely dependent on others. Imagine going from running a successful company to being unable to read the newspaper.

Work, in the traditional sense, was out of the question. Over time, Dave has regained at least some of his independence and has found meaning and purpose in his life. Most recently, his neighbours have discovered that a more determined worker is hard to find. They provide him with tasks around their yards that he can easily tackle, and he does so with a determination that is hard to beat.

This summer, while staying at my home in the country, Dave spent 3 solid days pulling thistles out of my yard by hand. 3 Days! He has a fierce sense of purpose, and accomplishes whatever he puts his mind to. He builds furniture by hand. He never takes for granted what he is able to accomplish since none of it comes easy to him and he is proud of himself when a job is well done. Though he exclaims that he "works all the time" with feigned exasperation, he loves it. We all need to feel as though we make a difference to someone else.

No matter how much some of us complain about our jobs, proclaim that we wish to retire and wish we could just stay home, for most it just isn't true. We all need to have a purpose, and to be truly happy that purpose has to take us outside of just providing for our own needs. It must extend to the outside world. Helping others makes us happy.

Slow Down - "Take it easy"

Dave doesn't rush. While this can be a frustrating quality for anyone in a hurry to go anywhere, you simply can't rush Dave. Because he has to concentrate intently to complete a task, Dave gives jobs his full attention. He works, speaks and drives slowly. He takes his time. David is never in a hurry.

The rest of us, on the other hand, seem to spend our lives perpetually rushed. We speed from one task to another, seldom present in the actual task at hand. This not only affects our actual productivity, it affects our stress levels and in turn, our happiness.

Taking time to enjoy the journey is a contributor to happiness. When we are rushed we aren't present. When we aren't present we aren't grateful. When we aren't grateful, we most often aren't happy.

Don't Worry - "Oh well"

Dave doesn't worry. Now to be fair he has little to worry about since his wife largely manages his day-to-day affairs. He is not responsible for paying the bills, opening the mail, getting the groceries, or "bringing home the bacon." He has no real responsibilities other than the ones that are self-imposed.

However, carefree moments are often happy moments and we can all learn to pay attention to and appreciate moments when our guard is down and we can be truly care-free. Though all of us carry the stress of responsibility to varying degrees, we do not need to stress constantly. That is a bad habit and one that can be broken with conscious effort.

The word happiness comes from the old English word "hap," as in "happenstance." At its root, the word refers to luck, a random joyful experience. I don't believe we can buy happiness, and longing for it just takes us out of gratitude. I do, however, believe we can take some lessons from Dave's life and simply "be". Be present, be grateful and be carefree. We can spend time in environments that nurture us and feed our souls. We can slow down and enjoy each moment that brings us joy. We can pay attention and be present to all that is good in our lives. We can choose to forget the lingering thoughts that disrupt our peace. In living a bit more simply, more like Dave, I believe we too can be happy.

Secrets to Happiness

By Angi Ma Wong

From ancient Chinese culture through to modern times, the lunisolar calendar has been consulted for agricultural purposes as well for birthdays, festival dates and celebration dates. In China, a person's traditional upbringing also included memorizing the twelve zodiac animals in Chinese astrology, just as we memorize the names of the twelve months of the year. Another essential was knowing the five components of one's destiny: fate, luck, Feng Shui, charity and philanthropy, and self-cultivation.

The first of these is fate, which includes all the circumstances of our birth, including era, family, ethnicity, status, socio-economic circumstances, etc. Next is luck, of which there are three kinds: heaven, pure, and man-made. Good heaven luck puts you before or after a terrible accident at a busy intersection while bad heaven luck places you in that accident. Pure luck is exactly that. An example is the woman from the Philippines who called her relatives to buy her one lottery ticket that won California's $134 million jackpot. Man-made luck results from your choices and decisions. The third component is Feng Shui, literally translated as Chinese for "wind-water." It is the ancient, natural, intuitive and holistic art of placement that aligns our energies with those of nature and the universe.

Charity and philanthropy is doing good deeds and sending out positive energy into the universe. It is karma and reaping what you sow. With money or love, the more you give, the more you receive, often in unexpected and surprising ways. The last tenet is self-cultivation and education - the constant evolution of one's self: personally and professionally, intellectually, physically, sexually, mentally, spiritually, and emotionally.

How do these five principles relate to the wisdom buffet offered here? The threads of the "braid" will unravel to reveal the beauty of hope and inspiration in this and subsequent chapters.

Considering that humankind has been around for up to 50,000 years, since the Paleolithic era, we are told, the idea of emotions is a relatively new idea. Our species was too occupied with survival for most of the time to even think about what we were feeling. Emotions? A little research revealed the shortest list had five: fear, anger, sadness, joy, and love. The longest compilation listed 85, but whichever you consult, joy/happiness is included on both.

But imagine, it was an upstart of a new

nation that had the audacity to actually include the concept of happiness in its constitution! Almost two and a half centuries later, is that idea flawed? Why should we be pursuing, as in chasing after, happiness? Can we feel or possess it naturally? A lot of people have it all wrong. While "life, liberty and the pursuit of happiness" is part of the United States Constitution, it does not guarantee happiness. You could run after happiness throughout your life and never find, reach or possess it.

Tony Robbins identified the six needs of people: certainty, variety, love, significance, growth, and contribution. Could it be that just meeting these six needs guarantees happiness? I think not, but instead believe that people who have just the three basic human needs of food, shelter and clothing can be content as well as happy.

A July 2013 TIME magazine cover

story, entitled "The Pursuit of Happiness," bears this out. A survey of the happiness quotient around the world found surprisingly that poverty, civil and drug wars, high employment rates, harsh weather, violence, and other negative conditions did not translate to unhappiness, but rather the opposite. Citizens in wealthy Singapore, which has an excellent education system and low unemployment, ranked very low on the happiness "meter." On the other hand, the people of Scandinavian countries, Mexico, Panama, Ireland, Brazil, Somalia, and Guatemala rated themselves above-average in being satisfied with their lives.

Being a 25-year cancer survivor who has undergone seven different chemotherapies and two radiation regimens in the past eight years, after cancer returned after 16 years, I've had a lot of time to think about being happy.

In my transformation over the years, it has been a wonderment to think about which of the five components of destiny have contributed to where I am now in life. My conclusion is that all of them have, each differently leading to various circumstances, just as the I-Ching, the ancient Chinese Book of Changes, states that every change in our lives is one of a possible 64.

The following form the essence and heart of my own happiness.

Be True to Yourself and Your Core Values

With age, maturity and experience, most of us find what is really important in our lives. We know what has value, both in ourselves and in other people, and we naturally gravitate toward those who share our values as life partners and friends.

Honesty, integrity, kindness, respect,

dependability, compassion, responsibility, caring, dignity, and decency are qualities of good character. They became the components of our personal compasses, fixed and unwavering as we grow older.

> *"Be yourself, everyone else is taken."*
> —Oscar Wilde

Don't try to be something or someone you are not. In the end, you may feel like a fraud or at least, discontent and unfulfilled as you pursue an elusive goal. During whichever stage or age you are at in life today, savor and enjoy the journey of discovering of what you care for and feel passionate about. Take time to discover and uncover each layer of your true uniqueness to find what makes you feel content, at peace with yourself, and happy.

Years ago, during my first cancer experience, I attended a support group meeting at which all attendees were asked to write a list of all the things that made us happy. We did not have to share the list, but were instructed to take it home, tape it on our bathroom mirrors and do at least two to six activities from it every day.

Imagine – even if you manage to do just one thing from the list that makes you happy, you will have done something for yourself each day. Make the time and effort to carve out personal time daily. Treat yourself, you're worth it!

Whether you take a daily walk, read, listen to music, watch a favorite show or movie, cook, play an instrument, take a class, soak in the tub, talk to a friend or family member on the telephone, do nothing for 30 minutes, or whatever makes you happy that is legal and not harmful to yourself or others, you are affirming that you are worthy of doing something special for yourself.

Of course you should do it, because you are special.

Doing these things, you will be recharged and re-energized. Without them, you may feel tired, resentful, burned out, deprived, bitter, depressed, or angry at yourself or others. Remember that if you keep giving and giving without replenishing your mind, body and spirit, it won't take long for you to scrape bottom.

Think of taking care of and being kind to yourself as refilling the pot, so to speak, so that you can continue to give to others. You are also affirming that you are deserving of the love of others as well, whatever your background, upbringing, or social or financial circumstances.

To be loved, we need to love and take care of ourselves first. Often that begins with forgiving ourselves and others for all real and imagined slights and hurts, past and present. You may be surprised to find that forgiveness is liberating and brings peace.

Ways To Be Rich

"There are two ways to be rich: work harder or desire less," proclaimed the message I read on a T-shirt in a Honolulu souvenir shop many years ago while on a hectic, island-hopping book tour.

We've probably all done it in our lives at some time or another because it is such a human thing to do – comparing ourselves, our conditions and our circumstances with those of others around us. Once you get seduced into counter-productive thinking or into the "rat race," it is difficult to pull out of it.

There will always be someone who has more of something than you do, and you can make yourself pretty miserable and bitter if you are always pushing yourself to attain what others have. While you're making comparisons, there are far more people who have less than you do.

Your life is not theirs, or vice versa. Everything about someone else's life and material wealth cannot be duplicated, even if you own exactly the same things. If you envy another's possessions, you will never be satisfied. If you are jealous of another person, you will leave yourself open to a plethora of negative emotions. You can keep working harder and longer for the remainder of your life and still not achieve.

"Those who want much are always much in need."

– Mohammed

It is more important to have what you need than what you want, as many during an economic depression or recession have found out. Working harder might not necessarily generate more income, merely more disappointment, anger or frustration, all of which are injurious to your health and relationships. Families have had to make very difficult and painful choices. When their lives are reduced to the basics, people around the world at every economic level discover what in their lives is truly worth having and keeping.

As Friedrich Nietzsche said, "Necessity is not a fact, but a matter of interpretation." What one person or family considers as basic needs represent luxuries to another. Designer clothing, vehicles, bottled water or going out to a movie don't even factor into the choices of a family that just needs to put food on the table or shoes on their children's feet.

By desiring less, your life can become easier and simpler. The simple act of divesting your life of unnecessary things can give you the feeling of greater freedom, empowerment and liberation. If you really want to feel rich, make a list of all the things you have that money can't buy. When was the last time you read the U.S. Constitution, the Bill of Rights and the ten amendments? Reflect on and appreciate your freedoms of speech, to vote, to assemble peaceably, of religion and to petition every day.

A recent AARP article about being thrifty revealed that for many "cheapskates," the formula was simple: spending less money created more time. Often, just delaying a purchase can diminish the desire to buy. If your children are clamoring for you to buy them something, ask them if they would spend their allowance or be willing to work to earn the money for it. Many things lose value when they are free and conversely, are treasured when a person's time, money or other resources are personally invested in their acquisition.

Now, ask yourself whether you would rather have wealth or good health? Can you enjoy your riches if you are not healthy?

Define Your Own Success

Many folks believe if they are successful, they will be happy, but it is not true. The news is filled with the latest tidbits about the fabulously wealthy or celebrities who are lonely, angry, bitter, friendless, miserable, physically or mentally ill, have addictions, or exhibit antisocial or destructive behavior.

While they may accumulate and surround themselves with status symbols that represent success and material wealth such as homes, cars, planes, jewelry, designer clothing and accessories, and so on, but they are spiritually impoverished. They may have all the money to spend on themselves and others, but may be stingy with spending it on others. They are not happy, content, or at peace with themselves or their lives.

On the other hand, there are those who

do not possess material wealth but are rich in the love of their family and friends and those who they respect. They are doing what they love and earn enough money to live modestly, simply or comfortably. They enjoy the satisfaction and contentment resulting from doing meaningful work of which they are proud, and living the life they want on their own terms.

"The greatest good you can do for others is not just to share your riches, but to reveal to them their own."

– Benjamin Disraeli

Don't waste another day feeling sorry for yourself or envying what others have. Wake up every morning and see each day for what it is – a gift and a new opportunity to take action and make change happen in your life and in your world. Or as Gandhi said, "Be the change you want to see in the world." This and the following two quotes are among my favorites because they go hand-in-hand.

"Love what you do and you will never work a day in your life."

– Confucius

"Happiness does not come from success. Success comes from happiness."

– Buddha

People who love what they do, live a life of love. By knowing yourself, you can explore and discover your purpose in life, and then live it with passion. Happy people are most likely also successful people, and success is what you define it to be, not how someone else perceives it to be, and more likely than not measured in the size of your bank account or assets.

As the old proverb goes: Go wake up your luck.

Whatever You Are, Be a Good One.

These wise words are from America's most popular and respected president, Abraham Lincoln.

Self-development means always reaching to a higher place to improve yourself. It is the process of challenging and cultivating yourself intellectually, mentally, physically, psychologically, and emotionally to evolve into a better human being.

"We must always, change, renew, rejuvenate ourselves, otherwise we harden."

– Goethe

Every one of us is special, one of a kind. What kinds of "smarts" do you possess? Yours are unique to you. How can and will you make the best of them? How high or far can you go?

Since the 1800s, there has developed a great

deal of interest and research in identifying
and quantifying what form intelligence
takes. In 1983, Dr. Howard Gardner of
Harvard University developed the idea
of multiple kinds of intelligence: spatial,
linguistic, logical-mathematical, kinesthetic,
musical, interpersonal, intrapersonal,
and naturalistic, added in 1999. Thomas
Armstrong put it in simpler language: space
smart, word smart, number/reasoning
smart, body smart, music smart, people
smart, self smart, and nature smart. Daniel
Goleman in 1994 developed the idea of
emotional intelligence – the concept of
self and social awareness, and self and
relationship management, critical for
advancement in today's fast-paced and
competitive world.

But the simplest and loveliest way I ever
heard intelligence explained came from a
teacher. When I told an elementary school
audience that I had math anxieties and was

technically-challenged, she told me, "Your head is filled with pictures and words, not numbers."

Your potential and possibilities are limitless. If you believe it, you can achieve it.

> *"It is never too late to be what you might have been."*
>
> – George Eliot

How May I Serve?

> *"This I know to be true. Only those of you who have sought and found a way to serve will be happy."*
>
> – Albert Schweitzer

Who is someone, living or dead, who you admire? Who is somebody you view as a role model? Who is a person you would tell, "I want to be like you when I grow up," no matter what your age is today?

There are heroes who live among us with whom we have contact every day. They are not necessarily known celebrities, very famous or wealthy, or people whose names are in the news. Examine the folks with whom you interact during a week's time and take a closer look. Think of how those people affect your life and you may be surprised. You may not have thought of a single parent raising children alone, a community volunteer, a colleague, a neighbor, a co-worker, a fellow club or church member, or even a member of your family.

You have the potential to be a role model or leader too. You don't have to consciously work to do so. Your life can be an example to others. By living your core values, you can be the person others would like to emulate.

Do everything with pride because your words, actions, and work comprise your calling card. Conduct yourself and your business with self-respect, honesty, and integrity. Expect excellence and the best from yourself and those around you. Maintain high standards but don't put pressure on yourself by demanding perfection from yourself or others. Consider that some things will never be accomplished if you wait for perfection.

> *"You can preach a better sermon with your life than with your lips."*
>
> –Oliver Goldsmith

You need not possess material riches to share them. To take the time to teach a child a skill that you know, to open his or her eyes to new things to appreciate the world or the environment, to help him experience something that affected your life in a positive way, or to help him realize and appreciate his blessings – this is the stuff of which role models are made.

As an adult, you can become a mentor, taking someone under your wing, guiding him or her in your profession, and giving that person the benefit of your knowledge, expertise and experience.

Outside your work or business, there are many skills that you can teach to others. There are countless community organizations that need volunteers to reach out to youth, the needy, seniors, and the less-fortunate. Take to heart the motto of Virginia Polytechnic Institute and State University: "Ut Prosim - That I May Serve" and make it your own.

Whether you give your time to a hands-on project or your attention to someone on a one-on-one basis, there will always be a person who will appreciate you. There is much to do in your own community and the opportunities for involvement are infinite. Most kindnesses do not involve giving money but your heart.

In the service of others, you can reclaim your soul or find your true self. Discover the reward and riches of giving unconditionally to make a difference in someone else's life. What can you think of that would benefit someone who is less fortunate than you?

"The greatest good you can do for others is not just to share your riches, but to reveal to them their own."

– Benjamin Disraeli

Live Each Moment Now

Over twenty-five years ago this spring, I was told that a lump in my breast was malignant. Upon returning home from a stay in the hospital for a lumpectomy, I walked through my front door and experienced an epiphany. In one glance, I saw my lovely home through new eyes. All of a sudden, it occurred to me that everything within my sight had less value than my family and friends. The furnishings and accessories, even the house itself, could never replace the love and support of those around me.

Immediately another realization dawned. Life was too precious and short to waste and there was no knowing how much longer my life would be. Cancer could have easily taken my life and by golly, I had things I had dreamed of doing, places to go and people to meet. It was at that very moment that I decided that I had better get moving to make those dreams real.

"When you look back on your life, you will regret the things you have not done more than those you did."

–H. Jackson Brown

Look around you, near and far, and it doesn't take much to see that most people are putting off their dreams. You hear folks saying things like, "When I retire, my husband (or wife) and I will_____," or "When I save this much money, I'll____."

The trouble with this line of thought is that life is unpredictable. From one moment to the next, we have no clue what it will bring. Right now you are enjoying a perfectly ordinary day but within the next few seconds, you could be downed by a heart attack or stroke, or lose a family member, friend or your job. Within minutes, a hurricane, earthquake, fire, tsunami, flood, a terrible disaster (remember 9/11?) or freak accident could strike.

I put the following words on our family's holiday card one year as well as used it in a Rotary speech, both times resulting in positive and poignant responses.

To realize the value of ten years:

Ask a newly divorced couple.

To realize the value of four years:

Ask a graduate.

To realize the value of one year:

Ask a student who has failed a final exam.

To realize the value of nine months:

Ask a mother who gave birth to a stillborn.

To realize the value of one month:

Ask a mother who has given birth to a premature baby.

To realize the value of one week:

Ask an editor of a weekly newspaper.

To realize the value of one hour:

Ask the lovers who are waiting to meet.

To realize the value of one minute:

Ask a person who has missed the train, bus or plane.

To realize the value of a second:

Ask a person who has survived an accident.

To realize the value of one millisecond:

Ask the person who has won a silver medal in the Olympics.

To realize the value of a friend:

Lose one.

Time waits for no one.

Treasure every moment you have.

– Author unknown

What Dreams Are You Putting Off?

Is it learning a new skill, taking your dream trip, reaching out for your dream job, or being your own boss as an entrepreneur and starting up your own business? Whatever it is, don't delay. Even doing something as simple as setting aside a jar with a "Trip Fund" label taped on to collect your spare change each night or setting up an automatic deposit from your paycheck into a savings account qualifies as your taking the first step.

Choose to be happy now and keep in your heart the words of Ralph Waldo Emerson:

"Write in your heart each morning that today is going to be the best in your life."

....

"Enjoy life. It's later than you think."

–Chinese proverb

Found in the Fall

By Jim Thomas

Over the years of ups and downs in my personal life, I came to realize a fundamental truth about being happy. This truth is tough to swallow for many people. Well, the fundamental truth I have found about being happy is that it's hard work. Being happy doesn't come shrink-wrapped in a cellophane package and when it's done, tossed in the trashcan. Being happy isn't about finding the weakest person and making fun of them. Happiness is not found at the big box stores. True happiness cannot be held in our hands, seen, tasted or touched. True happiness is a feeling that lies deep inside our mind's eye – it either burns bright and hot as the summer sun or dimly lit like the pilot-light glowing in the belly of a ready furnace.

Please allow me to tell you a story that changed

my life and helped me find my happiness.

It was the morning of November 11, 2011. I had been laid off work and was actively looking for a job. My wife's brother and sister were at our house and we just finished eating breakfast. It was about 9:30 a.m. and I decided to break away and clean the leaves off the roof while everyone else made plans for the day and cleaned the kitchen. I got the aluminum ladder from the garage and set it up on the frost-covered deck. My middle son came out and wanted to help me, so I collected the tools I needed and helped my son up to the roof. After he was sitting securely in place, I began to climb the rest of the way up. My right foot was on the roof and my left foot was still on the ladder. When I pushed from the ladder with my left foot to get onto the roof, the ladder began to slide on the frosty deck. My left foot didn't clear the top rung of the ladder – the rung grabbed my leg and took me down backwards.

The sound of the aluminum ladder crashing flat on the deck was immense – then a second boom even louder followed, filling the split-second silence as my back made contact with the top of the ladder from 8 feet in the air, also smashing my shin under the rung of the ladder at the same time.

I summoned all the strength I had to roll my body off the aluminum ladder onto the deck. My breath had escaped my lungs as I lay on my side, gasping for air. I heard our sliding glass door slam open, my wife yelled, "JIM! - DON'T MOVE!" and then I had the feeling I was going into a tunnel.

The morning sun gently glowed on my face as I blinked to see the warm yellow hues through the trees for the last time – then I closed my eyes to leave this body and peek into the next life.

All of a sudden a faint and calming inner voice – from my mind or elsewhere – said, "There is still so much more for you to do."

Slowly, I began to take shallow breaths. Opening my eyes with a renewed "I'M ALIVE" awakening, I looked at the sun once again and felt its slight warmth on that cold November morning.

The first order of business was to take an inventory of what was hurting. My left shin and back became the main focuses of pain.

The thought of being paralyzed didn't cross my mind. "No – not today," I said internally. I commanded my toes to move. Nothing happened. Fire pulsating deep in my back, again I commanded my toes to do as I willed. "Move, damn it," I mentally yelled as loud as I could from within my mind. Finally, my toes began to twitch – I knew the connection was made from my brain to my toes and everything was going to be okay.

My wife's voice broke through my internal thoughts and I heard her say, "Don't move, Jim! You're going to be okay. Don't move."

Our most dire moments in life are where we'll find true happiness. The simple movement of my toes awoke a spirit I had never before experienced in my life. I pray you will not find happiness in neither place nor predicament, but when all other options are removed and God gives you a gift to keep going, live to the fullest. Let other people experience the joy and love you feel. I am grateful with every breath, every blink, and every heartbeat. My intention for this book is to share with you stories and experiences to warm your heart and hopefully find the happiness of life.

The Kindness of Strangers

Before coming home from the five-day

hospital stay with a broken back, bruised shin bone and swollen feet, I was told my road to full recovery would be 12 months. I was offered the choice to either have back surgery with steel pins and rods or wear an extremely uncomfortable brace for 12 weeks any time I was vertical. The doctor was one of the best orthopedic spine surgeons in the area and told me most men are unable to wear the brace and end up going to surgery. Go figure – men. My wife, by my side, said, "Jim, will not be in those statistics and I will see to it." And she did.

I owe my wife so much. She helped me recover from this accident to the point that I can never repay her. She never asked for a thank-you and never complained even once. Her positive spirit fed my soul and gave me the strength I needed to become well again. Thank you so much, Katie.

When we arrived home from the hospital, I

laid or sat, trying to be comfortable in our home. I was out of work, and we had no income coming into our home. We had no idea how we would deal with the financial burdens we faced, but we agreed to remain positive and together no matter what.

As the day went on and in my hazy fog of medication, we were completely surprised by the outpouring from our community. Neighbors, some I had never met, all came to our home and began working to clean the leaves from the roof and gutters, raking the yard, and taking care of all the outside chores. There must have been 10-15 people all over, working in unison as I peeked out the window with tears in my eyes.

Then, the doorbell rang and in came some neighbor ladies. All had food in their arms, telling us to not worry about anything but getting better and healing. We had never met several of them, but they came to us by word of mouth from our generous neighbor across the street to offer support to this young family of six.

As my pain and discomfort began to grow, my wife helped me to our bed where I laid – dozing off and on continuously day after day. The doorbell continued to ring as word traveled around the community. Strangers would stop by with gift cards and checks for us to pay the utility bills and buy groceries for Thanksgiving. We were unable to thank them enough for their generosity.

One day, just before Thanksgiving, the phone rang and my wife was in another room and didn't hear it.

The cordless was on my bed within reach so I answered. The caller ID read a person I didn't know.

"Hello," I said.

"Is this Jim?" the voice asked.

"Yes."

"I heard about your accident from your neighbor, who is a good friend of my wife's and I was told to stop by your home for a few minutes."

I said, although not too level-headed, "Well, that's fine; I'll need to ask my wife. What time?"

His reply: "Now – I'm right outside your house."

"Okay," I said and hung up.

I was able to get my wife's attention, explain to her the brief phone call as she helped put my brace on, and get my cane in time for the doorbell to ring. Mr. "X" introduced himself to her and she showed him into the living room. I had already found my chair next to the fireplace, close to the warmth. He introduced himself to me, shook my hand and took a seat across the way.

My wife recognized his last name and asked if he was related to an auto dealer with several establishments around St. Louis. He replied, yes. He was the founder of the business and his children run the company now. We chatted for a little about whom he knew and the connections that brought him to us. Katie has a way with relationships – she knows no stranger. Mr. "X" then told us the reason he was there: he wanted to make a contribution to us directly. He asked a few more questions and then stood, saying it was wonderful to meet us good people, then asked Katie to borrow an ink pen. She retrieved the pen and they stood at the kitchen table while he wrote and chatted about what had happened. He folded the check and gave it to Katie. They exchanged hugs, he told me to get better and get well, and then he and

Katie walked together as she saw him out.

Katie came back in as I was heading back to bed to rest. She opened the check and it read, "Get well soon," with a five-thousand-dollar amount written on the check.

Our eyes swelled with tears of joy, knowing that everything would be okay. To us, Mr. "X" was an angel that appeared in our most desperate time of need to offer us help when we needed it most. His kindness and generosity kept our family together and reassured us that if we kept the faith – even when times were at their most difficult stage – everything would work out.

Over the next six weeks, we saw the same generosity and support from people all over – our immediate family had never seen anything like it before in their lifetime. A miracle was taking place before everyone's eyes that year.

Stoke the Love and Feel the Happiness

Four weeks after the accident, Katie and I went to doctor's office where we received great news – the healing was coming along nicely. On the way home from the doctor's office we decided to get some lunch at Red Robin – a tasty burger shop – cane in hand and Katie by my side. The place was fairly busy with shoppers as there is a mall close by. You could feel Christmas in the air as we entered. Katie and I got a booth by the window and began discussing the past, present and future, like most couples do. We started talking about a book we read earlier in the year, called The Power by Rhonda Byrne.

Byrne made reference to a time in her life when she was broke, and instead of worrying, she used her strong belief in the law of attraction and withdrew her last $200.00 and walked down the sidewalk looking at people in their eyes with the intention of giving it to one of them. She told the story of how it made her swell up with so much joy and happiness that it was indescribably the most exciting event in her life.

I asked Katie, since we had been blessed with so much, if we should do something similar. It was a week before Christmas and it would be a great present to someone if we could buy their lunch. Katie agreed enthusiastically and we set out looking around the restaurant for someone to secretly receive our gift.

We spotted a young couple in a two-person booth; they seemed happy about life. Nothing stood out about them particularly, but Katie and I agreed that those were the people we would buy lunch for. We motioned for our waiter and told him about our plan. We asked him not to say anything about the bill until they are ready to go and don't tell them who did it. We would pick up the tab; just tell them, "Merry Christmas." Our young waiter said, "Okay," with a little smile of apprehension and curiosity on how this was going to play out.

Our waiter did what we asked and communicated our message to the couple's waitress without telling them who was actually paying for their meal.

Katie and I sat quietly and nonchalantly eating our lunch, watching as our self-produced real-life movie was about to unfold before our eyes. The couple completed their meal and motioned their waitress over to retrieve their bill. Their waitress had a big smile, walked over, and told them, "Someone here has paid for your meal and they wanted me to tell you, Merry Christmas."

The smile from the young couple's faces was huge and priceless! They looked around the room for anyone who would have done it and begged the waitress to point us out, but the waitress didn't know, either.

The girl was completely taken back by someone buying them a meal and began whispering to other patrons if they did it.

They replied, "Did what?"

"Pay for our meal!" she said with a big smile.

"No," they said, smiling.

"We didn't either," another table offered.

"No, we didn't," yet another said, smiling.

Within a minute, everyone in the restaurant was turning their heads talking about who had done this generous deed. It was like Christmas morning for older people.

The young couple told their waitress, "Tell them, thank you."

The waitress replied, "I believe you already did." Laughter erupted.

They remained seated and whispered to each other, looking around. They stayed for about 10 more minutes trying to figure out what had just happened. The girl was bound and determined to find out who paid for their meal. Katie and I were looking over, but didn't acknowledge our secret Santa gift.

Then, the young couple motioned their waitress over again, giving her their credit card while whispering something to her. By this time, we didn't know what was happening, our waiter glanced over at us, and we looked at him, but not long enough to draw attention to us.

The young couple received their credit card back, signed it, and got up – still smiling and looking around for anyone suspicious. They put their coats on, and waved goodbye to all their new restaurant friends. "Merry Christmas," they said and walked out.

Patrons were still laughing, smiling and talking about what had just happened and trying to make sense of it all.

Katie and I looked at each other thinking, "What just happened?"

Our waiter came over to us – big smile – "I've never seen that before!"

We started chatting back and forth, laughing and having fun. It was so cool and fun to watch. We were the only three people who knew the secret in the whole restaurant. We had so much fun seeing the excitement and happiness in the room, and we felt like we did our job to make people happy as everyone was laughing like children. Plus, it was an experience like no other.

Our waiter left to attend to his other tables. Katie and I were discussing the event to each other, laughing amongst ourselves and reliving the last brief moments. A few other patrons close by had figured out it was us. Everyone was cracking up over the couple's reaction.

About a minute later, a guy walks up to Katie and me. He wasn't there to deliver the bill. It was more than that, as we could tell from the look on his face. Smiling, he asked if it was us who paid the bill for the couple. We said yes, thinking it was fun to see the young couple's reaction.

The man was smiling and shook our hands. He then got more serious and said, "What happened there gives me hope for humanity. This proves there are really good people out there. You guys doing that taught my girls a valuable lesson of kindness."

Our waiter came back to us and he stood

next to the gentleman after speaking to the young couple's waitress. The man then went on to say, "That young couple just paid for our meal, too." The waiter chimed in – confirming the man's words by shaking his head and saying, "They sure did."

The seriousness of the gentleman's face became apparent, saying, "You have no idea what you did to help us, thank you so much." We didn't want to pry into the man's meaning; sometimes it's better not to overanalyze.

Katie and I had no intention of turning our lunch into a theater, but it sure was fun. Actually, it had more drama, excitement, happiness and pure enjoyment than any other entertainment we had ever personally experienced. Complete strangers were caught off guard and shared a meal together as if they'd known each other forever – priceless memories.

If you haven't felt the overwhelming joy of giving away money to people who didn't ask for it, or buying a meal for complete strangers – you haven't lived yet. You can actually FEEL your heart swell up to the point of weeping with happiness. Give it a try – you'll be hooked.

The Wisdom Buffet Writers Biographies

Janet Mitsui Brown

Janet is a life-long artist. She is an author/ illustrator of a children's book entitled Thanksgiving at Obaachan's, a columnist in two Southern California online news journals, Culver City Crossroads & California Crusader News, and a published writer in the Los Angeles Times, the Los Angeles based Rafu Shimpo newspaper, and other journals.

Janet is also the co-owner of Tani B Productions, Inc., a film/publishing production company, and its subsidiary The Joy of Feng Shui, where she is the principal practitioner, advising individuals and businesses on how to enhance their lives utilizing Feng Shui principles.

Janet is a tai chi international gold medalist, and continues to study with the Wushu Center in Los Angeles and Hanzhou, China. Janet formally studies Feng Shui with Helen

& James Jay at Feng Shui Designs, Master Larry Sang of the American Feng Shui Institute, and His Holiness Grandmaster Lin Yun and Her Holiness Khadro Crystal Chu Rinpoche and their disciples, with the Yun Lin Temple.

Based on her experiences, Janet offers consultations in tai chi gong, feng shui, and meditation. Her writings on these subjects can be viewed on her website, and in her ongoing news columns. Janet works with her husband, actor Roger A. Brown, and her daughter Tani, a writer, formerly with Google, and presently a Fulbright Scholar in Southeast Asia.

Katherine Graham

Katherine Graham is a Lifestyle Enhancer and Modern Feng Shui Practitioner based in Atlanta, Georgia. Katherine is known for her powerful, practical and personalized approach to Classical Feng Shui. She is currently writing her first book on Feng Shui, due out in 2015. Connect with Katherine on Facebook and Twitter under Haven Feng Shui, which is also the name of her private Feng Shui consulting company. And, if you're interested in reading about Classical Feng Shui with a Western twist, check out her blog titled, Feng Shui for the Type A where Katherine shares her Feng Shui tips and expounds on her motto: "Dismiss Dogma, Seek Results."

Mary Jane Kasliner

Mary Jane Kasliner graduated from Skidmore College with a degree in Health Science and Union College with a degree in Applied Sciences. After nearly 20 years of being a health care practitioner, Mary Jane decided to shift her focus to the disciplines of feng shui and yoga.

She studied Western Feng Shui at the De Amicis School in Philadelphia and Classical Feng Shui at both the New York School of Feng Shui and Feng Shui Institute of London. In 2008 Mary Jane finished her 200 hour national teacher training program in Hatha Yoga at the Center of Health and Healing and Personal Revolution Baron Baptiste program at Yoga Bliss. Several years afterwards, she completed her Mastery of Meditation teacher training program under Master Anmol Mehta.

In 2005 she opened Body Space Alignment,

a feng shui and yoga consulting company. Her clients include some of Manhattan's elite. She later established the Teaching Tortoise School of Feng Shui that offers certifications in Classical Feng Shui.

In 2009, Mary Jane was part of Seane Corn's Off the Mat and Into The World Humanitarian effort to Uganda. Mary Jane raised thousands of dollars for orphaned children due to war and AIDS in Uganda.

Mary Jane has received world-wide media coverage from the Associated Press for her work. She has been interviewed on TV and radio many times and is the author of 3 books, 15 Feng Shui training CD's, and a Feng Shui design CD.

Located in Ocean, New Jersey, Mary Jane loves to play golf and travel whenever she can. Mary Jane can be contacted at www.fengshuiyoganj.com.

Kim Klein

Kim's background is in the healing arts, with areas of study ranging from Massage Therapy to Chinese Medicine. Later, as a student of the Rhodec International School of Interior Design, she became acutely aware of the difference in an environment that looks good ascetically as opposed to an environment that actually nourishes our well-being. She started reading every book she could find on the subject of Feng Shui and then attended and graduated from the three year BTB (Black Tantric Buddhist) Masters Training Program, studying the teachings of Professor Lin Yun under teachers Steven Post, Barry Gordon and Edgar Sung. She has also attended many advanced Feng Shui workshops by various teachers, including Seann Xenja, Richard Feather Anderson, Roger Green and others.

Kim is an award-winning author and has written ongoing Feng Shui columns for several newspapers, including the Napa Valley Register and the Santa Barbara NewsPress. She has authored a variety of very popular blogs, including The Coffee Shop Diary along with co-publishing her first novel and screenplay, Nine Degrees North, in March of 2013. Kim recently finished her second screenplay, Twenty-One Sunsets. Her passion for writing is complemented by her experience in a variety of fields, such as Feng Shui, Chinese medicine, multi-media art and design. She is currently working on a novel, Letters From York and has a book in the works about Feng Shui combined with other modalities, entitled Life by Design - creating and living the life you desire.

Located in Santa Barbara, California, Kim currently practices as a Certified Feng Shui Consultant, working with both residential and corporate environments. She is also a Certified Health Coach and has clients ranging from the Napa Valley to Miami. (Kim Klein, www.kimkleinfengshui.com, or on Facebook at, Kim Klein Fusion Feng Shui.

Belinda Mendoza

Belinda Mendoza is a certified Feng Shui consultant trained in the US and China in East and West Schools of Feng Shui with Professor Lin Yin, Jon Sandifer and Raymond Lo. She is also a Reiki Master and applies energy work to all her consultations.

Belinda is a graduate of the University of Texas at Austin and a former social worker and corporate sales leader. She left those professions and began her Feng Shui business in 2000. She is a problem solver and has been helping businesses and people create positive change in their lives through feng shui analysis, redesigns, staging and space clearing for over 17 yrs.

Her passion is her yorkies and she runs a monthly dog group for 7 years helping owners socialize their pets. Belinda has a new book published through Hay House called, "Feng Shui For The Loss of a Pet, Restoring Balance during Grief and Loss, A Personal Journey".

Belinda is also a Big Sister in the BBS program for 9 yrs. now. She can be reached at www.designforenergy.com or belinda@ designforenergy.com.

Belinda resides in Austin, Texas and always offers a free 30 minute phone consultation for anyone interested in Feng Shui or her services. 512-740-1251. She wishes you Fortunate Blessings!

Mia Staysko

Mia is a professional Feng Shui consultant, artist and designer. Through her company, White Lotus Interiors, she helps people to create spaces that support their bodies, and their souls. Mia's goal is to help people to transform their lives and their spaces through conscious design.

Mia is certified in BTB Feng Shui, studying with His Holiness Grandmaster Lin Yun, Katherine Metz, James Jay and David Kennedy. She has additionally studied traditional Chinese methods, Flying Stars Feng Shui, 4 Pillars Astrology, 9 Star Ki and BaZi with Jon Sandifer and Dr. David Lai. Mia has a keen interest in yoga, numerology and all things spirit-lifting.

Mia is the founding Director of the Sacred Lotus School of Feng Shui and an active member of the International Feng Shui Guild.

Mia blogs on design, Feng Shui and other uplifting topics at www.livingfengshui.ca and produces the digital Living Feng Shui Magazine.

James (Jim) Thomas, MBA

Jim has become a successful small business entrepreneur who continues to build and grow businesses. His specialty is computer science however, he went back to school to receive a masters degree in business administration, then became a feng shui consultant.

Jim and Katie own www.fengshuiemporium.com, www.luckycat.com, and www.fengshuidirectory.com. Jim also saw a great opportunity with Amazon/Kindle Publishing and contacted other feng shui authors for help writing this series of books. The collaboration of authors are known as The Wisdom Buffet Writers.

Jim enjoys spending time at his home in Missouri, family, friends as well as his customers from around the world. He loves hiking, water sports, traveling, and exercising.

A special thanks goes to his wife, Katie

and his kids, the love of his life. Jim's business coach, Shawn Chhabra, who has guided and helped his business knowledge and to his family and friends for their unwavering love and support.

Angi Ma Wong

The daughter of a diplomat who grew up in New Zealand, Taiwan, NY/NJ, Washington, D.C., finally settling in Los Angeles, her namesake city. Angi started five businesses in 1989, including being a publisher/author and an intercultural and Feng Shui consultant to over 200 real estate developers globally, hundreds of individuals, diverse business and industry clients.

She is the award-winning and best-selling author of 28 titles, including 15 on Feng Shui such as her best-selling Feng Shui Dos and Taboos series, as well as inspirational, children's, historical and business books. Her Survivor's Secrets to Health & Happiness is a four-book award-winner.

Known as the Feng Shui Lady (R), Angi has appeared on OPRAH, Regis, Redbook, PEOPLE, TIME and over 600 print, broadcast and internet features, and is one of the few Asian Americans on the global speaking circuit on a variety of topics.

Visit Us

<u>www.TheWisdomBuffet.com</u>

www.ingramcontent.com/pod-product-compliance
Lightning Source LLC
LaVergne TN
LVHW020354090426
835511LV00041B/3125